Powerful Planning Skills

Envisioning the Future and Making It Happpen

Written by Peter Capezio

POWERFUL PLANNING SKILLS

Envisioning the Future and Making It Happen

By Peter Capezio

CAREER PRESS–Franklin Lakes, NJ

POWERFUL PLANNING SKILLS
Cover design by Barry Littman
Printed in the U.S.A. by Book-mart Press

To order this title, please call toll-free 1-800-CAREER-1 (NJ and Canada: 201-848-0310) to order using VISA or MasterCard, or for further information on books from Career Press.

The Career Press, Inc., 3 Tice Road, PO Box 687, Franklin Lakes, NJ 07417

Career Press endorses nonsexist language. In an effort to make this handbook clear, consistent, and easy to read, we have used "he" throughout the odd-numbered chapters, and "she" throughout the even-numbered chapters. The copy is not intended to be sexist.

Library of Congress Cataloging-in-Publication Data

Capezio, Peter, 1947-

Powerful planning skills : envisioning the future and making it happen / by Peter Capezio.
p. cm.
Includes index.
ISBN 1-56414-441-0 (paper)
1. Business planning. I. Title.

HD30.28 .C374 1999
658.4'012—dc21 99-056825

Table of Contents

INTRODUCTION

How to use this handbook

Congratulations — you have taken the first step toward improving your planning skills by purchasing this handbook! Here's how to get the most out of it:

1. Briefly review the entire handbook. Get familiar with the type of information that is presented.

2. Use the handbook as a reference guide. Look up what you need, when you need it.

This handbook contains many planning tips and techniques. Planning skills are always needed — for organizing, for projects, for prioritizing — so take this handbook with you when you change jobs or assignments. Whether or not your job calls for supervising people, good planning skills will improve your effectiveness. If you do supervise others, you will benefit from passing on your planning skills to the people who work for you!

When a guided missile is launched, it has a final destination imprinted on its memory. This information alone, however, is not enough to ensure that it will hit its target. The wind, air pressure and other forces slightly affect the missile's direction and speed. In order to stay on track and on target, it frequently communicates back to the launch unit and asks (in computer language), "Am I on target?" In response, the launch unit tells the guided missile to alter its course "a little this way and a little that way" (in computer language again, of course). Throughout the journey, the guided missile alters its course hundreds of times. Having done so, it hits the target perfectly most of the time. Had it not frequently asked, "Am I on target?" it would not have had a very good chance of completing its mission successfully. So it is with your projects — without careful planning and follow up, the likelihood of getting your mission accomplished turns into mission impossible!

1 HOW DOES PLANNING IMPACT MY SUCCESS

"To do great, important tasks, two things are necessary: a plan and not quite enough time."

— Anonymous

The Nature of Planning

Planning is defined as the act or process of making or carrying out the establishment of goals, policies, and procedures for a unit of work.

Unfortunately, people don't talk or think about planning too much, and planning skills are generally only mentioned when they are poor or sorely inadequate. However, a lack of planning often causes a project to fail because *"Changes occur that were not anticipated."* You may recall how bad planning has gotten you into binds and jams. *"Unrealistic time lines result in stress for you, and they make customers unhappy when you miss a deadline."* Or incomplete plans may rob you of successfully reaching your goal. *"The lack of a contingency or backup plan left you scrambling when your original plan fell through."*

Good planning skills may not be the hot topic at the office water cooler, but perhaps they should be. Planning skills are *survival skills* for busy people because they are necessary to see a successful conclusion to a project. Planning skills enable you to *chart* the course of a project, *steer* it toward completion, and *focus* on your vision and goals like a laser beam. With good plans you can prioritize tasks, minimize waste, and capitalize on opportunities that come your way.

Planning skills require the *logical evaluation* of projects or problems. Logic tells you to look at things in *broad-to-narrow* terms. When planning a project you must look at the overall goal, the broad ramifications, and the resources that you need. Then, as you define the broad picture, a more detailed analysis will naturally follow. Good planners don't forget either the "big picture" or the details. Several tips and techniques on broad-to-narrow planning will appear in following chapters.

Your plans form a *foundation* for how you approach your work. This foundation can be either strong or weak. A strong foundation is a building block for success, while a weak foundation hinders your success.

Planning Helps You Do More with Less

When was the last time you were told that you had as much time as you wanted to complete a project? Have you ever been told that you had unlimited resources to accomplish a job? Are you able to staff extra employees to cover peaks in your workload? Should quality ever be compromised for meeting a quota?

If you answered "never," "not in this lifetime," "certainly not," and "no way" to these questions, you are not alone. At some point in time we all have been asked to cut expenses, produce faster, and/or increase customer satisfaction. The reality of today's business climate is that you need to do more with less.

How Does Planning Impact My Success

Unfortunately, you probably will be asked to do more with less *many times* in the future. Tomorrow's successful employees will be the ones who have come to terms with this challenging climate and have *planned for it*. Consider the following examples:

- "The budget numbers just came in, and we need to cut our payroll ..."
- "Our biggest client wants us to improve our turnaround to two days without it affecting his prices ..."
- "Two loaders just called in sick, and it's too late to call anyone to cover for them ..."
- "We are at a critical point in the project, where making a wrong decision can throw us off course ..."

Sound familiar? Now consider some of the planning skills you need to deal with these challenges:

- "The budget numbers just came in, and we need to cut our payroll ..."

  Planning skills: forecasting, prioritizing, Pareto analysis.

- "Our biggest client wants us to improve our turnaround to two days without it affecting his prices ..."

  Planning skills: systems and process analysis, setting objectives, strategic planning.

- "Two loaders just called in sick, and it's too late to call anyone to cover for them ..."

Planning skills: contingency planning, redefinition of work tasks, checking for progress.

- "We are at a critical point in the project, where making a wrong decision can throw us off course ..."

  Planning skills: definition of vision and goals, critical path analysis, simulation (visioning).

These and other planning skills allow you to better handle the tough demands that you face. By learning to do more with less, you will better manage the changes to come. (See Chapter 6.)

Your Planning Skills Influence the Productivity of Others

Consider the following statement: *You are responsible for making yourself and others around you more successful and productive.* If you believe this statement, you need to understand the impact that your planning skills have on your work environment. It should come as no surprise that the better you plan, the more successful you and those around you will likely be.

The more effectively you plan your work, the more clearly your employees will understand what's expected of them. A lack of clear responsibilities and goals is frustrating and puts them at a disadvantage. Before you begin a new project or assignment, you should give a great deal of thought to how it will impact others. Because whenever there are changes in the workplace, a reevaluation is needed. Employees need to know how any changes will affect what they are doing.

In addition to helping define roles and responsibilities, good planning helps prioritize activities. Without an upfront analysis of your work, you might prioritize based on "who screams the loudest." But when you plan the work up front, you look at how each action will impact the organization and how much flexibility you can build into each component of the plan. Good planning allows you to make better decisions when prioritizing. You can make your group more productive by anticipating potential shortages and/or problems and by taking action to compensate for them in advance. This sense of order during chaos allows your employees to better handle last-minute changes.

You have already read how good planning skills positively affect what you are working on today. However, they also help shape how you and your employees approach future projects, assignments, and problem-solving efforts. In other words, *the things you do today set a precedent for what you will do tomorrow*. If you set high standards for quality and performance on current projects, you are more likely to get top quality and superior performance on other projects. When you expect a lot from others, expect the same from yourself. In other words, set a good example. Your good planning skills will rub off on your co-workers and subordinates!

Think of the supervisors and managers whom you admire and respect. What skills make them successful? Chances are they are good at analyzing their work. Chances are they are good planners. If you plan well, you will likely be admired and respected by others too. The following accolades are all tied to the ability to plan.

- "He's got his act together."
- "He seems to think of everything."

- "He reacts well in the face of adversity."
- "His group seems to be very focused."
- "They're able to see the big picture at all times."
- "His projects are executed very intelligently."
- "He can handle changes well."

Good planning can make you look like you are always on top of the situation. As a result, you should be among those getting the most challenging projects, the best assignments, and the most frequent promotions!

Take Your Planning Skills with You

The good news is that planning skills are basic to all types of business. As your career progresses, you will continue to rely on the skills you have used so far *plus* develop new ones. Your development should be shaped by both how well you benchmark your successes and how well you learn from your failures.

When you start a new job or want to reevaluate your current position, take an inventory of the planning skills you will need vs. the skills you already have mastered. The following planning skills inventory will help you determine what needs to be developed, and the remaining chapters of this handbook will show you how to do it.

Planning Skills Inventory

Planning Skill	Importance 1-10, 10 = very important	Skill Level 1-10, 10 = highly skilled
Understanding the vision		
Developing a vision		
Defining project goals		
Setting objectives		
Brainstorming ideas		
Getting others involved in the analysis		
Forecasting		
Contingency planning		
Progress reviews		
Follow-up		
Process improvement		
Day-to-day detail management		
Strategic planning		
Developing trend-setting plans		
Dehassling the workplace		
Change management		
Time management		
Presenting plans		
Tools of analysis		
Bouncing back when things go wrong		

Reflections

Chapter Summary

Planning skills are survival skills. Your plans form a foundation for how you approach your work. Planning also helps you do more with less. When you plan, you should look at projects in broad-to-narrow terms.

Your planning skills affect the productivity of others by establishing clear roles and responsibilities, and by helping everyone prioritize more effectively. By using good planning skills today, you will help yourself and your employees prepare for the future and, at the same time, instill good planning habits in everyone.

People notice good planning skills, so you will be perceived as more successful if you plan well. And because planning skills are needed at all levels of any organization, you should evaluate your skills as your career progresses.

2 YOUR PERSONAL PLANNING STYLE

"We are what we repeatedly do."

— Aristotle

No two people approach planning in the same way. Each person is unique in the way she approaches organizing and analyzing her work and work environment. Your own style determines which areas of planning will be "second nature" to you and those that will be more baffling.

The better you understand your personal style(s), the better you will be at developing the planning skills you need at each stage of your career. Self-awareness can make you more successful by helping you identify what planning activities you are likely to have more trouble completing.

When it comes to planning, there are four main behavioral types: the Perfectionist, the Chaotic, the Trendsetter, and the Referencer. To determine your basic style(s), take the short assessment that follows. You'll find interpretations for each style after the assessment.

Assessment instructions: Circle the word or phrase that best describes you and/or the way you behave at work. You should circle one of the words/phrases per line.

Section A:

	Column 1	Column 2
1.	Step by step	All at once
2.	Calm under pressure	Emotional under pressure
3.	Slow but steady	Fast and tense
4.	Average sense of urgency	High sense of urgency
5.	Patient	Impatient
6.	Like to concentrate on one	Like to have lots of things going on at once
7.	Rattled by sudden changes	Unaffected by sudden changes
8.	Persuaded by facts	Persuaded by emotional content
9.	Precise	Exciting
10.	Use detailed daily planner	Use "Post-It" notes and/or a less detailed planner

Total circled in Column 1: ______

Total circled in Column 2: ______

Section B:

Column 3	**Column 4**
1. Detail-oriented	Big-picture-oriented
2. Fact-based	Logic-based
3. Like to compare with the past	Hate to compare the with the past
4. Do a lot of research	Do what makes sense
5. Seek backup to theories	Rely on personal expertise to make decisions
6. Take some time to make decisions	Make quick decisions
7. Implementer	Entrepreneur
8. Defensive	Stubborn
9. Self-critical	Self-confident
10. Flawless	May leave out a few details

Total circled in Column 3: ______

Total circled in Column 4: ______

Assessment Interpretation

- If you circled six or more in Column 1, you have PERFECTIONIST tendencies.
- If you circled six or more in Column 2, you have CHAOTIC tendencies.
- If you circled six or more in Column 3, you have REFERENCER tendencies.
- If you circled six or more in Column 4, you have TREND-SETTER tendencies.

Write your two strongest tendencies here:

____________________   ____________________

If you're a Perfectionist

Strengths: The Perfectionist is the most methodical of the four styles. You tend to have good organizational skills. You prefer to take on one project at a time. Others perceive your work as very precise and of high quality.

Potential weaknesses: The Perfectionist may have trouble accepting rapid changes in the workplace. Be sure that you are "in the loop" so that you know when change is coming and you can plan for it. As a Perfectionist, you can get frustrated when asked to juggle many things at once.

Developmental tips: Take a change-management course, develop a way for you to handle many tasks at once methodically, and make sure that you have open communication lines with your manager.

Example: *"I was just told that I'll be heading up the relocation project. First I'm going to lay out a master plan* *and then begin looking at each individual area that must be moved. I've then got to delegate some of my other projects so that I can concentrate on this. I certainly hope they don't change things on me in midstream like they did on the last project — what a tense time that was!"*

If you're a Chaotic

Strengths: The Chaotic is the most dynamic of the four styles. You prefer to take on many projects at a time. You have a tremendous sense of urgency and unlimited energy. Others perceive your work as very persuasive and interesting.

Potential weaknesses: The Chaotic may have trouble focusing on one project at a time, so be sure that you don't recommend change just for the sake of change. The Chaotic also can get bored and lose attention easily.

Developmental tips: Take a time-management course, develop your ability to be more patient, and minimize distractions when working on high-priority tasks.

Example: *"I was just told that I'll be heading up the relocation project. What a great opportunity this is! They say I should delegate some of the other projects that I'm working on, but I don't think I'll need to. Life will just be a little crazier over the next few months, and I can handle it. I certainly hope they let me go at my own pace. The last project I did took twice as much time as it should have because I had to wait for other departments to do their share of the work. What a hassle!"*

If you're a Referencer

Strengths: The Referencer is the most detail-oriented of the four styles. You tend to view things in "micro" terms, leaving little out. You prefer to do an evaluation or get approval before making a decision. Others perceive your work as very exacting and thorough.

Potential weaknesses: The Referencer may have trouble seeing the big picture and, therefore, get bogged down in the details. Because Referencers hate to fail, they may take too much time analyzing alternatives, so time schedules may suffer. Referencers also may become defensive when others critique their plans.

Developmental tips: Take a risk-management course, keep the broad goals or objectives of your plan posted in front of your work area so you can see them often and try to positively accept feedback to minimize your defensiveness.

Example: *"I was just told that I'll be heading up the relocation project. There is so much to do, so many elements. I've already made an initial list of 30 individual tasks that need to get done. I certainly hope they take the time to explain to me what they want. On the last project I had a hard time figuring out what to do and how to do it — no one took the time to review it with me."*

If you're a Trendsetter

Strengths: The Trendsetter is the most innovative of the four styles. You tend to generate lots of ideas when brainstorming alternatives for a plan. You are very confident and decisive. Others perceive your work as visionary and antibureaucratic.

Potential weaknesses: The Trendsetter may have trouble accepting other people's ideas and may be stubborn. Because Trendsetters are less detail-oriented, they may make decisions without looking at all the angles. The Trendsetter also can get frustrated when asked to stick to the "status quo."

Developmental tips: Take a project-management course, develop your need for attention to detail and allow others to contribute suggestions before you make your final decision.

Example: *"I was just told that I'll be heading up the relocation project. This should be fun. I'm already thinking about how I'm going to approach it. I certainly hope they let me be creative and take a few risks on this one. On the last project they wouldn't leave me alone and let me do my job. It was frustrating."*

Combinations

If you're a Perfectionist and a Referencer

If you fall under both of these styles, then you probably are regarded as a "flawless implementer" at work. The work you do gets done right, as specified, and completely.

Developmental tips: Concentrate on seeing the big picture and on change management.

Example: *"I was just told that I'll be heading up the relocation project. They said that I need to make decisions a little quicker this time, that I spent too much time collecting data on my last project. I don't know about that — I think it's important to be sure first. The last project I did was perfectly thought out and implemented, and that takes time."*

If you're a Chaotic and a Trendsetter

If you fall under both of these styles, then you probably are perceived as a charming and persuasive entrepreneur. You have a passion for new ways and new things.

Developmental tips: Concentrate on managing details and learning patience.

Example: *"I was just told that I'll be heading up the relocation project. They said that I need to involve others and not be so eager to try something completely new. Apparently, my last project wasn't 'mainstream' enough. Hey, but that's progress, right? What's more important — doing the right thing or feeling comfortable about it?"*

Assessment interpretations

If you circled six or more words/phrases in one column, it does not mean that you do not have any of the qualities contained in the columns for which you circled four or fewer words/phrases. In fact, you may have behavioral tendencies for all of the types; however, they will be more dominant where you circled the most words/phrases.

Actions to take to develop your planning skills

Determine two to four personal development goals based on your assessment results and what you've learned about yourself. Use the assessment interpretations with the "Planning Skills Inventory" (in Chapter 1) to provide you with ideas.

Example:

Development Goal: I have very strong Trendsetter tendencies and would like to develop my attention to details.

Action to take: Plan time to review details of each project.

Action to take: Bounce my ideas off Sam; he's detail-oriented.

Action to take: Attend a project planning course.

Development Goal # 1:____________________

Action to take: _________________________

Action to take: _________________________

Action to take: _________________________

Development Goal # 2:____________________

Action to take: _________________________

Action to take: _________________________

Action to take: _________________________

Development Goal # 3:____________________

Action to take: _________________________

Action to take: _________________________

Action to take: _________________________

Chapter Summary

We are all unique in the way we approach planning. There are four main behavioral planning types: the Perfectionist, the Chaotic, the Referencer, and the Trendsetter. Some people are a combination of these. Your style determines how you approach situations and projects. Understanding your personal planning style will help you focus your development efforts.

3 TYPES OF PLANS

"Chance favors the prepared mind."

— Louis Pasteur

The reality of having to "do more with less" may lead you to become more reactive than proactive. You simply won't have the time to spend planning *future* projects! The good news is that certain types of plans allow you to plan more for the future by simplifying the management of your work *today*.

For example, planning can be focused on the broad needs of the business (strategic planning), the very detailed nature of your day-to-day needs (personal planning) or on specific projects (single-use plans). Additionally, you can use many preestablished plans to help you manage your work in a consistent manner (standing plans).

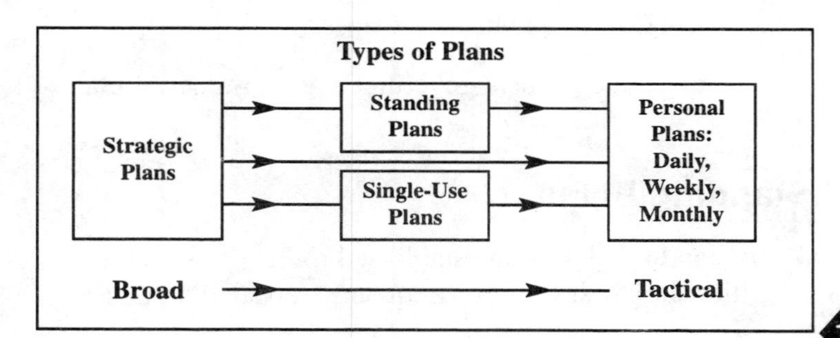

Strategic Planning

Strategic plans tend to be long-range. They involve an analysis of the work environment, the economic issues, the trends and the existing competition. The intent of a strategic plan is to shape the future of your organization, either totally or partially. You should base your department's strategic plan and your own goals on those of the overall organization, then develop personal plans to accomplish these goals.

In the regular course of business, you should study the long-range plans of your company or division and consider how they impact your work. Strategic plans are the basis for developing operating plans, which outline how your business or department is run on a daily basis. Operating plans usually take the form of either standing or single-use plans.

Benefits of a strategic plan

- Establishes a vision for the organization
- Sets the overall direction
- Serves to unite divisions or departments under a single, overall mission

Examples of strategic plans

- Three-year training plan
- Corporate business plan
- State or local government urban-renewal plan

Standing Plans

A standing plan is an established routine or set of activities. It is best used for frequently repeated tasks. For example, if you have ever been asked to set a work policy or procedure, then you have developed a standing plan.

Benefits of a standing plan

- Greatly simplifies work that needs to be done over and over again
- Standardizes actions
- Gives employees a general guideline to follow (they don't have to start from scratch each time they do an activity)
- Takes advantage of lessons learned in past experiences

Examples of standing plans

- Policies and procedures
- Training plans
- Scheduling
- Production plans
- Performance-evaluation plans
- Safety plans
- Order-processing plans

Situational or Single-Use Plans

A single-use plan is a one-time plan developed for a single purpose. It is best used for unique projects. The nature and importance of the project will determine how much time you should spend on it. Single-use plans are often developed as part of a major change taking place in your business or department. Because the situations and components are unique, data collection and contingency planning are especially important.

Benefits of a single-use plan

- Brings structure and predictability to organizational changes
- Customizes actions to fit a particular situation or event
- Ensures accuracy because data collection is tailored to the plan's overall purpose or goal
- Helps busy people manage their work demands with focus and confidence

Examples of single-use plans

- Budgets
- Reorganization plans
- Special-event schedules
- Problem-solving plans
- Implementation plans for a new policy (these may become a standing plan)
- New computer-systems implementations
- Most projects
- Process-improvement projects

Personal Planning: Daily/Weekly/Monthly

Along with project planning, personal planning skills have a tremendous impact on your productivity. Personal planning refers to the upfront thought and action you put into organizing your personal work. In other words, it's how efficiently you bring together your daily responsibilities and other special projects. In order to do more with less, busy people need skills to organize and prioritize their work.

There are as many approaches to personal planning as there are types of busy people! The key to getting your work life organized is *doing what makes sense for you.* Here are some organizational dos and don'ts:

- *Don't* try to lock yourself into a very detailed and elaborate organizational system if you're not naturally detail-oriented. You'll get frustrated and probably not use the system anyway.
- *Don't* use "Post-It" notes and scraps of paper to keep track of your activities if you need a more structured approach.
- *Do* find an organizational system that complements your style and meets your needs. Some people find it easier to make weekly planning objectives with daily to-do lists that tie into their weekly goals, while others prefer to set monthly goals with weekly and/or daily checklists. There are, of course, some people who don't like checklists or setting goals at all!

Again, the point is not how you organize but that you do it in a way that makes the most sense to you and that fits your personal style. Here are some questions to ask yourself to determine how you should approach getting organized.

1. On which time period should I focus — by project milestone or on a monthly, weekly or daily basis?
2. What special organizational needs do I have?
3. What tools can I use to prioritize?
4. What type of organizational tools best suit my personal style — daily planners, wall calendars, checklists, etc.?
5. How can I change my organizing habits in order to become more productive and maintain my sanity?
6. What have I learned from the past about organizing my work?
7. Should I delegate more? (Ask for feedback from your peers and your manager. Perhaps you can become better organized by delegating tasks you don't do well or don't have time for.)

"Getting organized is no end in itself; it is a means to get where you want to be."

— Stephanie Winston
The Organized Executive

"In your daily planner, there should be a place for your personal mission statement so that you can constantly refer to it. There also needs to be a place for both your roles and short-term and long-term goals."

— Stephen Covey
The 7 Habits of Highly Effective People

ARE YOU ORGANIZED?

Instructions: Answer the following questions to determine how organized you are.

1. How often do you forget meetings or appointments?

   ____Never ____Seldom ____Sometimes
   ____Often ____Always

   Why?____

2. How often do you find yourself shuffling through piles of papers to get information that you need right away?

   ____Never ____Seldom ____Sometimes
   ____Often ____Always

3. Could you update your manager on the status of all your projects or assignments if he walked up to you right now?

   _____Yes _____No

   Why or why not?______________________________

4. Would your peers say that you are an organized person?

   _____Yes _____No

   Why or why not?______________________________

5. How often have your projects been completed on time (over the past year or so)?

   ____Never ____Seldom ____Sometimes
   ____Often ____Always

For those that were not completed on time, what caused the delay?

____

Reflections

Interpretation

Each of the previous questions will help you determine how organized you really are. The following questions will help you diagnose your developmental needs.

1. Which of your answers are you most concerned about? Why?

   ____

   ____

2. What aspect of organizing is most difficult for you? Why?

   ____

   ____

3. How does your ability to organize (or lack of) impact your work?

   ____

   ____

4. What organizational skill would you like to develop further? What action(s) should you take to develop in this area?

   ____

   ____

Now map out a development plan using what you have learned about your organizational skills. Of course, you will need to determine what actions will help you get better organized. Then establish weekly goals to track your progress!

Plan of action

What I'm going to do: ______________________

When I'm going to do it: ____________________

What measurement I will use: ________________

Case Study

Now that you've learned about the different types of plans, read this case study and determine what actions should be taken. A set of questions follows.

Sandra is a new supervisor of a sales department. She has been hired by the company because of her excellent sales background and her local contacts. Her new company would like to double sales in this department over the next year or so.

This is Sandra's first supervisory assignment. She feels confident about her management skills and is looking forward to her new career. Most of the people in her department have been working for the company for several years and know what they're doing. Looking at their individual files, Sandra notices that the vast majority of the employees were rated very good on their last performance reviews. Based on this information, Sandra determines that little direction is needed from her.

Over the next few months Sandra holds several meetings to talk about the need to increase sales. Several ideas are discussed, although no formal plans are ever presented. Instead, Sandra puts in many hours trying to make additional sales herself.

During her six-month review, Sandra's manager, Jack, delivers some bad news. The department's sales have gone down 5 percent! When Jack asks Sandra for an explanation, she replies, "I don't understand. I gave the group several new ideas for getting new customers, but I don't know why they are not using them!"

Case study questions

1. What has Sandra neglected to do?
2. Why do you think Sandra has resisted developing a formal sales improvement plan?
3. What difficulty is Sandra having that many new supervisors experience? Why?
4. What should Sandra tell Jack at this point?
5. What should Sandra say to her staff? How will she get her employees to commit to what needs to be accomplished?
6. What type of plan should Sandra develop?

Possible answers

1. What has Sandra neglected to do?

   Sandra has neglected to provide the group with a plan for improving sales. As a result, her employees are unfocused and unclear about what is expected of them and what they should do.

2. Why do you think Sandra has resisted developing a formal sales improvement plan?

   Because Sandra is a new supervisor, she does not realize the importance of planning skills — how they relate to her work and the work of her employees. She assumes that since the employees know what they are doing they will "read her mind" and do the right thing. Even good employees need to understand their goals and objectives.

3. What difficulty is Sandra having that many new supervisors experience? Why?

   Sandra is having a problem making the transition from line employee to supervisor. She has gone back to what she feels comfortable doing — selling. Many first-time supervisors go through the same experience.

4. What should Sandra tell Jack at this point?

   Sandra should ask for Jack's advice and admit that she has not been giving the group much direction. Perhaps he can help her come up with a plan for improving sales and for developing her own supervisory skills!

5. What should Sandra say to her staff? How will she get her employees to commit to what needs to be accomplished?

   Sandra needs to be honest with her people. She should admit that she has not given them the direction and leadership that they need, that they have a tremendous challenge ahead of them and that she needs their help in developing a plan for improving sales.

6. What type of plan should Sandra develop?

   Sandra should develop a single-use plan.

Chapter Summary

There are several types of plans: strategic, standing, single-use and personal. Strategic plans are generally long-range and more broad in scope. Standing plans are used for day-to-day or well-established activities. Single-use plans are best for special projects and making changes. Personal plans bring together your daily responsibilities in order to complete assigned projects. Organizational skills are critical for all types of planning, especially good personal plans.

4 THE BASICS OF PLANNING

"Plans are nothing; planning is everything."

— Dwight D. Eisenhower

Plans ensure that your overall desired purpose will be achieved effectively and efficiently. According to Chris Macdonald, author of *The Productive Supervisor*, "To begin a work assignment or project of any size or complexity without the productive resources and information you will need — that is, without *planning* it — is to run the high risk of failure."

Although each situation is different, there are common planning elements that you can use for most situations. This chapter reviews the basic elements of planning and how they fit into the overall process model.

The Planning Process Model

(for single-use plans)

The planning process is both linear and cyclical. It is linear because certain actions must be done in a certain order. For example, the overall purpose must be defined prior to data collection. It is cyclical because you must frequently refer to your defined purpose or goal to evaluate your progress. Also, you may need to return to previous steps of the planning process if you find that they no longer support the overall purpose. In general, the following steps show how you might typically move through the planning process, assuming there are no major glitches!

Steps in the Planning Process

1. Define the overall purpose or goal.
2. Determine the major components or objectives of the plan.
3. Make sure that your objectives align with (support) the overall purpose.

4. Collect and evaluate the data you will need to determine what it will take to complete each component of the plan.

5. Make sure that the data you collected and evaluated supports the overall purpose.

6. Develop a forecast plan.

7. Make sure that your forecast plan supports the overall purpose.

8. Determine action steps.

9. Make sure that your action steps support the overall purpose.

10. Develop contingency plans.

11. Make sure that your contingency plans support the overall purpose.

12. Implement your plan.

13. Make sure that your implementation supports the overall purpose.

14. Check the progress of your plan frequently.

15. Make sure as your plan is implemented that the overall purpose remains in focus.

Seems like a lot of steps! In reality, you will find that taking a few moments to focus on the plan's overall purpose will *save you time over the life of your project*. Much more time is wasted reworking project plans when halfway through you discover that the project is off course or does not support the overall goal.

Now let's look at each component of the planning process model in more detail.

Define the Purpose or Goal

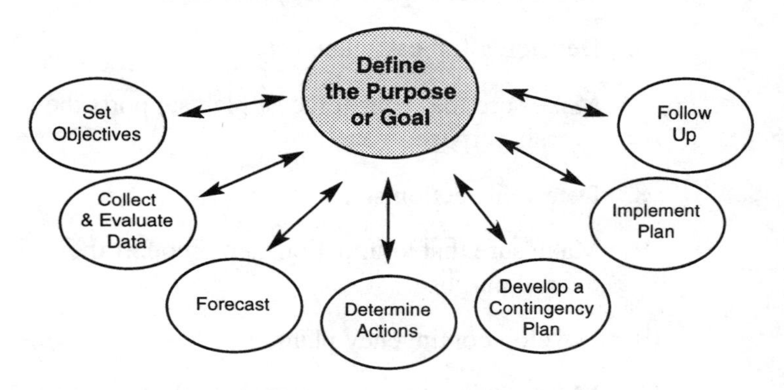

What: Ironically, this first and most crucial step is often the most forgotten. For any plan to be successful you must have a clear understanding of the desired outcome. So until the overall purpose is understood, nothing else should be done. As the model shows, you return to the purpose or goal between each step of the planning process to ensure that you are on the right track. Many well-intended plans go awry because people lose sight of the overall goal.

How: A well-defined purpose or goal takes some thought. Here are some of the main elements:

1. It states in *broad terms* what the desired outcome is.
2. It defines the project's time schedule.
3. It describes the resources that will be used. Resources should be expressed in terms of people's time and financial costs, among others.

4. It states any quality standards that are applicable (general accounting practices, customer satisfaction guidelines, no negative impact on other processes, etc.).

Example: Becky's work group wants to be ISO 9000 certified. To become certified, the processes that are used in the department must be documented, fully understood and used. Becky is in charge of the plan. The purpose or goal is to "become ISO 9000 certified within six months using 25 percent of three workers' time and no more than $10,000."

During the next few months, the work of documenting the department's processes begins. As this happens, it becomes clear that many of the procedures currently used could be improved. *Here's the critical point in Becky's plan.* If she returns to the purpose of the plan, *to become ISO 9000 certified*, she will have to redirect the efforts of those wanting to improve the processes to simply documenting them. In this case, process improvement is a separate goal that should be examined at a later time. ISO 9000 certification can be achieved with the current processes. If Becky does not return to her original purpose, then she and her team will get sidetracked by process improvements, meaning it will take more time and money to become ISO 9000 certified.

Becky also has the option of changing the purpose of the project to include process improvements; however, she will need to make adjustments to the certification time schedule and budget. Perhaps her department's processes are so outdated that improvements must be made as documentation takes place. If that's the case, then Becky must rephrase her purpose to include process improvement and ISO 9000 certification. Her plan also must reflect the longer time lines and greater resources that are needed.

What is bottom line, as shown in this example? Daily activities should reflect your overall purpose. That is how you stay on track to meet your goals. If defining your purpose or goal is so important, then why is it so often left out? There are three possible reasons:

1. People often think they understand the issue and move right to taking action. Although you may be able to immediately assess your own point of view, you need the perspective of others for your initial analysis.

2. When faced with pressing business problems, people often think they cannot take time for proper planning. Again, the tendency is to move directly to implementing the plan, without ensuring that your actions are aligned with the needs of your organization. In reality, planning saves time by reducing the need for rework.

3. If the planning styles exercise in Chapter 2 indicated that you tend to be a Perfectionist or a Referencer, you may move too quickly through the big-picture phase of planning and go right to the details. You need to look at the broad picture in order to ensure that the goals of the project are clearly understood prior to determining individual action steps.

Develop a purpose or goal statement

Exercise: Think of a project you are currently involved in or one in which you will be involved. Using the four elements of a good purpose or goal statement as a guide, develop a statement that fits your project.

___

___

Set Objectives

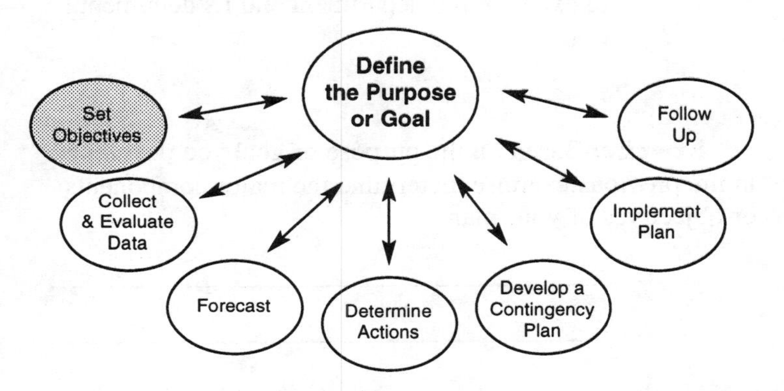

What: Based on your well-defined purpose or goal, you will want to set broad objectives that describe the major components of your project. Make a list of your broad objectives for easy reference.

How: You want to move from your overall purpose or goal statement to the details of your project. Do this by determining the major "chunks" of the project.

Example: In order for Becky's department to gain ISO 9000 certification, here are the major components of her project:

1. Determine which processes are already documented.
2. Document remaining processes as needed.
3. Communicate the processes to the people who work with them.
4. Perform internal audits to ensure that the processes are being followed.
5. Make needed adjustments.

6. Arrange for the outside certification company to examine the department and its documentation.

Exercise: Based on the purpose or goal you developed in the previous exercise, determine the major components or objectives of your plan.

1. ______________________________
2. ______________________________
3. ______________________________
4. ______________________________
5. ______________________________

Collect and Evaluate Data

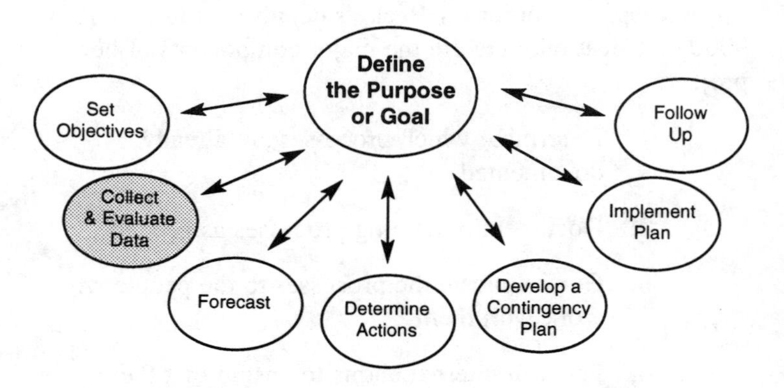

What: Once your broad objectives are set, data collection begins. For each major component of your project you need to determine what the relevant facts are and what actions are necessary to complete each objective. Then develop a realistic and factual list of specific details or critical success factors for each objective of your plan.

Be sure to involve others throughout the planning process, but especially at this point. You need feedback from people who will implement the objectives or be affected by them. By involving others now, you may prevent many problems down the road, where they are much harder to fix.

How: To collect the data needed for each objective, you should ask and answer the following questions:

1. What work is required to accomplish this objective?

2. Who must perform this work?

3. What issues or challenges will arise while getting this work done?

4. Are those involved committed to this project?

5. How long has similar work taken?

6. What is a realistic amount of time to complete this objective?

7. Are there any risks involved?

There are several tools you may want to use for collecting data. (Refer to Chapter 8 for specifics on check sheets, Pareto analysis and flow charts.) Again, make sure that your analysis supports your overall purpose or goal statement.

A note on risk: The future is always more or less uncertain. You reduce the degree of uncertainty — the risk — when you collect the relevant data and apply it to your forecast, which is the next planning step.

Example: Becky has collected the following data for her department's plan for achieving ISO 9000 certification.

Objective: *Document the remaining processes.*

1. What work is required to accomplish this objective?

   Thirty-eight of the department's 55 processes must be documented.

2. Who must perform this work?

   Each worker will need to participate in documenting the processes that she regularly does.

3. What issues or challenges will arise while getting this work done?

   The department is very busy. Taking the time to document the processes will be challenging for everyone. Several processes will be difficult to document because several versions are currently used.

4. Are those involved committed to this project?

   While Becky and her supervisors are committed to becoming ISO 9000 certified, the other workers don't see the need for it. They view certification as a lot of extra work.

5. How long has similar work taken?

   Becky's department is the third in the company to seek ISO 9000 certification. It took approximately three months for the other two departments to complete their documentation.

6. What is a realistic amount of time to complete this objective?

   Becky feels that documenting the remaining processes should take no more than three months, given the department's current workload.

7. Are there any risks involved?

   Becky's department faces losing customers if it does not receive ISO 9000 certification within the next year. During the last few months, several of the department's largest customers have inquired about its certification status. If the remaining thirty-eight processes are not documented, the certification process cannot continue.

Exercise: Based on two of the major objectives you identified in the previous exercise, complete the following data collection questions:

Objective: ______________________________

1. What work is required to accomplish this objective?

   ____

2. Who must perform this work?

   ____

3. What issues or challenges will arise while getting this work done?

   ____

4. Are those involved committed to this project?

   ____

5. How long has similar work taken?

   ____

6. What is a realistic amount of time to complete this objective?

   ____

7. Are there any risks involved?

   ____

Objective: ______________________________

1. What work is required to accomplish this objective?

____

2. Who must perform this work?

____

3. What issues or challenges will arise while getting this work done?

____

4. Are those involved committed to this project?

____

5. How long has similar work taken?

____

6. What is a realistic amount of time to complete this objective?

____

7. Are there any risks involved?

____

Develop a Forecast

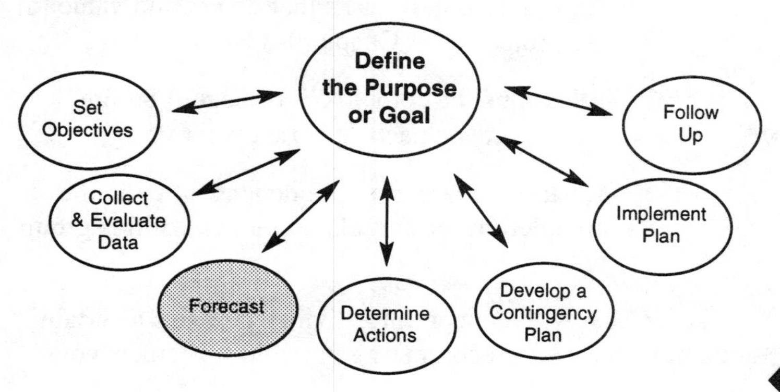

What: Forecasting is perhaps the most creative step of the planning process, because several views must be tested before you decide on a project schedule. At this point in the plan, all of your data should be integrated into a cohesive road map. Now you will take this detailed information for each objective and test how it works together in meeting the overall purpose or goal. This step is called forecasting because it is the first time that you will have information available to predict the project's schedule, the resources needed and necessary quality measurements.

At this point the feasibility of your purpose or goal statement may be challenged. Questions about timing or resources generally will surface as you look at each major chunk of the project and see how it relates to the other chunks. At the end of this planning step you will have a detailed schedule of activities — some that need to be done in a linear fashion and some that can be done concurrently.

How: Forecasting will be less difficult if you compare different possible scenarios to find the schedule that best meets the needs of the overall purpose or goal. To make a schedule for each major component of the project, answer these three questions:

1. Which activities must be done? Eliminate any duplicate tasks or tasks that do not add value to the project. (See Chapter 8.)

2. What must be completed (or begun) before work starts on each specific objective?

3. What other activities are dependent upon the completion (or partial completion) of this group of activities?

A forecast with concurrent activities contains a certain amount of risk. When comparing possible schedules, your analysis should include a risk assessment. Weigh the possible benefits against the possible costs and possible contingency actions. The more information you have about each objective, the better prepared you will be to assess the possible risks.

Unrealistic plans can create more problems than they solve! To determine if your plan is realistic, follow these three steps:

1. Have a trusted peer play devil's advocate.
2. Evaluate how your plan will impact other departmental plans.
3. Involve others — get their input!

Example: In Becky's plan to get her work group ISO 9000 certified, she makes a schedule using a Gantt chart, which is explained in more detail in Chapter 8.

This first project time line is based on a strictly linear progression of activities, with each task being fully com-

Project Time Line (in months)

	Month 1	Month 2	Month 3	Month 4	Month 5	Month 6	Month 7
Determine which processes are documented (3 wks.)							
Document processes (3 mo.)							
Communicate the elements of each process (1 mo.)							
Do internal audits (1 mo.)							
Make adjustments (1 mo.)							
Work with outside certification company (2 wks.)							

pleted before the next one begins. Notice that the estimated project completion time is seven and a half months. But Becky's purpose statement said that she wanted to have the project completed in six months! Before changing the purpose statement to reflect a longer completion date, Becky should look at the possibility of doing some of the activities at the same time. Here's a new time line that shows more concurrent activities.

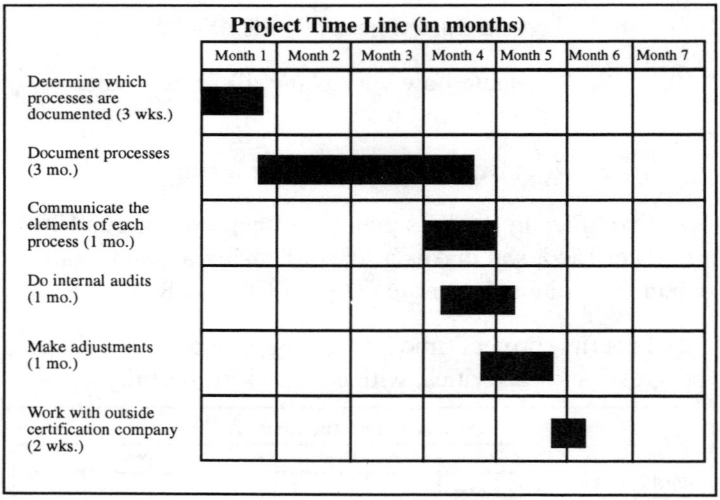

Project Time Line (in months)

	Month 1	Month 2	Month 3	Month 4	Month 5	Month 6	Month 7
Determine which processes are documented (3 wks.)							
Document processes (3 mo.)							
Communicate the elements of each process (1 mo.)							
Do internal audits (1 mo.)							
Make adjustments (1 mo.)							
Work with outside certification company (2 wks.)							

Notice that the project components themselves do not take any less time; rather, many are done concurrently. For example, while some processes are being documented, those already completed can be communicated. And as processes are communicated, individual audits can be done and adjustments can be made. The only major components of the plan that remain strictly linear are the first and last. Nothing else can really happen until Becky determines which processes need to be documented. And her department must finish all of its work before the outside certification company arrives.

Based on this new, concurrent schedule, the project can be completed in less than six months. Now Becky's job is to make sure that the plan is feasible. She needs to confirm that she has kept the broad goal in mind while ensuring that the people involved in implementing the plan can perform their activities based on her forecast.

Exercise: Develop a forecast based on the plan you have been working with in previous exercises. Develop it using this blank Gantt chart. A set of questions follows.

Objectives/tasks	Project Time Line (in ________)						

Exercise questions

1. Is your forecast realistic?

2. Are the activities in your forecast done one at a time or concurrently?

3. Does your forecast include all the major activities that must be done?

4. If you handed your forecast to a co-worker, would she clearly understand when activities

should be worked on and when the project will be completed?

Determine Action Steps

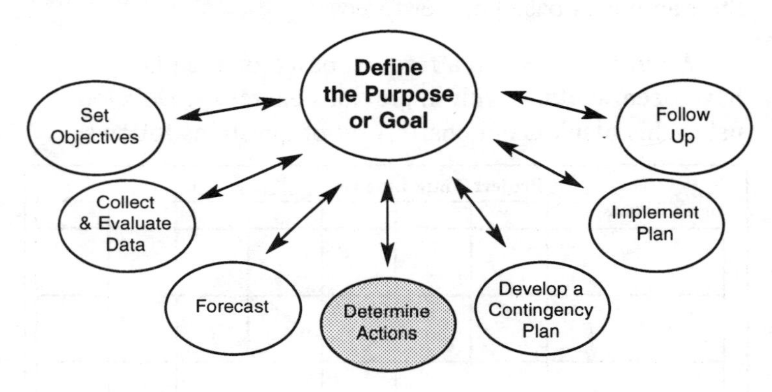

What: Based on your forecast and the details you gathered during data collection, determine what tactical steps need to be taken and in what order. During this part of the planning process, activities are defined in a very detailed manner. Eventually, you will develop detailed daily, weekly, and/or monthly activity checklists, and/or action plans. (Chapter 8 contains more information on developing an action plan.)

How: The key to success during this part of the planning process is not leaving anything out! As simple as this may seem, the tiniest forgotten step may sometimes stall an entire project. Depending on the nature of your project, you may want to develop daily or weekly checklists. There are countless ways that you can do this; however, you will want to use a format that makes the most sense for your project. Here are a few sample approaches:

1. Use daily checklists that tie into weekly check-lists and/or weekly checklists that tie into monthly tracking sheets for your action plan.

2. Keep all activities and their due dates listed on a master action plan.

3. Maintain individual checklists for each employ-ee.

4. Post checklists with all employees' names and their assigned responsibilities. (Peer pressure is a great motivator.)

5. Take advantage of project management soft-ware to track the completion of activities.

Example: Following is Becky's approach to determin-ing and tracking the action steps needed for her depart-ment's plan to become ISO 9000 certified.

Action Plan					
Project: ISO 9000 Certification				Project Leader: Becky	
Overall Purpose: To become ISO 9000 certified within six months, using 25 percent of three workers' time and no more than $10,000.					
Step No.	Action Step	Start	End	Measurement Criteria	Responsibility of
1	Review and communicate plan	11/13	11/18	Group agreement of understanding	Becky J.
2	Determine which processes need to documented	11/18	12/1	Satisfactory internal audit	Becky J.
3	Document processes (order area)	12/3		Satisfactory internal audit	Dora P.
3	Document processes (billing)	12/3		Satisfactory internal audit	John J.
3	Document processes (other).	12/3		Satisfactory internal audit	Sam Y.

1. Becky develops a master action plan that identifies the work that has to be done, by whom and by when. She organizes the actions both by objective and by time.

2. Becky develops individual checklists for each person that identify the work that needs to be done in more detail than on her master action plan. She sits down with each employee and reviews the master action plan and the individual's checklist. Then she asks for that employee's commitment to do the work.

3. Becky uses project management software to tie the individual checklists into her master action plan. When changes are made, both documents are updated and electronically mailed to everyone as part of a status report.

Exercise: Determine your action plan. Recall some of the action plans you have used in the past.

What worked well? ______________________________

Why? ____

What didn't work so well? ______________________

Why? ____

Action Plan					
Project:				Project Leader:	
Overall Purpose:					
Step No.	Action Step	Start	End	Measurement Criteria	Responsibility of

Develop a Contingency Plan

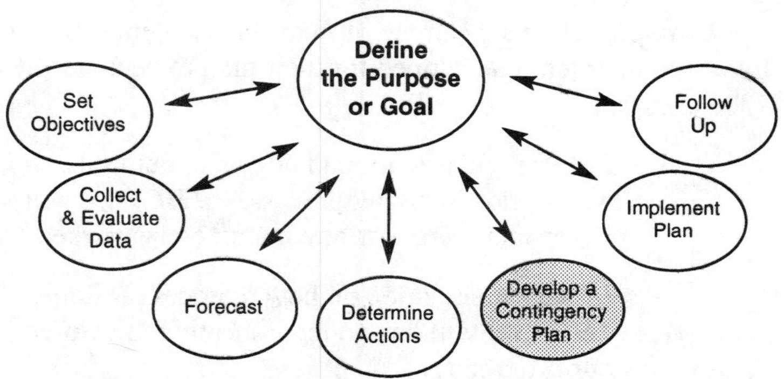

What: A contingency plan represents your efforts to guess what might go wrong or differently with your plan and how to handle it if it does. Developing a contingency plan is important because things rarely go exactly as planned. With a contingency plan in place, you can minimize the negative effects that changes may have on the success of your project. A contingency plan consists of several if/then statements that list what changes you will make to your plan if certain situations occur.

How: Coming up with these possible situations requires brainstorming. (See Chapter 8 for tips on brainstorming.) Be sure to involve several people in the brainstorming session and answer the following questions:

- What could happen differently from how we have predicted?
- What effect, if any, will these differences have?
- How should we deal with these differences if they occur?

Develop if/then statements for those situations that are either most likely to occur or those that will do the most damage if they occur.

Example: Here's a sample of the if/then statements Becky and her team developed for their plan to become ISO 9000 certified.

- *IF* our regular workload begins to get in the way of documenting processes, *THEN* we will either reprioritize or hire a temporary worker.
- *IF* we cannot agree on how a process is done, *THEN* we will have a team meeting to resolve our differences.
- *IF* we don't receive certification on our first attempt, *THEN* we will reapply within three months.

Exercise: Develop contingency plans for your project. Based on the purpose and objectives you have developed in the previous exercises in this chapter, brainstorm a couple of *what ifs*. In other words, do your best to predict what might go wrong. Complete the if/then statements by deciding what you would do if something undesired happens.

Example: IF our budget gets cut, THEN we will limit our use of temporary help and do the documentation binders in-house.

IF__________________ THEN________________

IF__________________ THEN________________

IF__________________ THEN________________

IF__________________ THEN________________

Implement the Plan

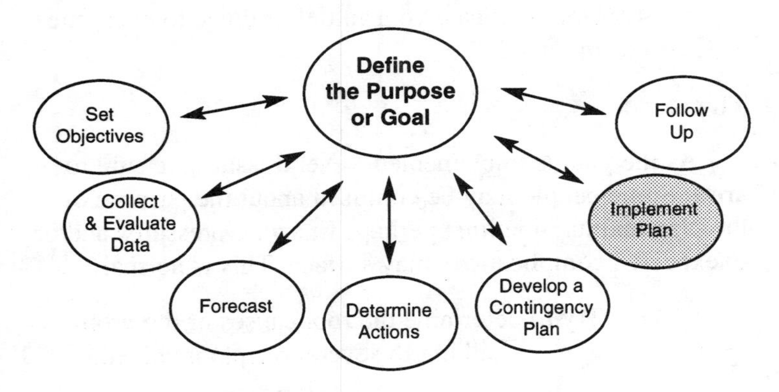

What: By this time, implementing your plan should not be like taking a plunge into the unknown. You've done your research, you've consulted with other people, and you have remained focused on your overall desired outcome or purpose. Now, take your forecast, action plan, checklists, contingency plans and begin.

How: Plan implementation has three phases: the start, the storm, and maintain and sustain. You must be aware of how these three phases will impact your plan's success.

The start

Follow these steps to begin your plan implementation.

1. Communicate the plan. Make sure that everyone involved clearly understands the overall purpose and the roles she will play in the implementation.
2. Track the initial activities very closely.
3. Get feedback from those who are involved. Are there any activities that need to be changed or added?
4. Communicate your initial findings to everyone involved.

The storm

As the plan is implemented, several issues are sure to arise. Some people may be confused about the purpose of the plan and its time line; perhaps financial pressures and/or unexpected complications may surface. This is normal.

1. Try to determine the root causes of the problems by talking to several people involved.
2. Make several small but needed adjustments. Look at ways of clarifying the plan so that small "irritants" don't get in the way.
3. Don't hesitate to implement your contingency plans if necessary.
4. Communicate, communicate, communicate.

Plans often stall due to a lack of communication or conflicting messages.

Maintain/sustain

As the initial focus and attention on the plan die down a bit, the people involved may become complacent or less motivated. It is important to keep up that momentum until the plan is fully implemented.

1. Space out any fanfare or special events connected to your plan. If you hold a big kickoff rally for your plan and then don't have milestone rallies along the way, people will sense that the project's importance has dwindled.

2. Be a role model — make sure that your motivation doesn't wane either!

3. Develop creative ways to keep the plan in everyone's mind. For example, use periodic memos with status information and graphics, post charts, leave phone or computer messages with reminders, updates, etc.

Example: Here's how Becky implements her plan.

The start

1. Becky holds a team meeting to explain the ISO 9000 certification plan in detail. She also calls short daily update meetings for the first couple of weeks. The master plan is posted on the department's bulletin board.

2. Each person has an individual checklist. The department's master plan is updated as activities are completed on each person's checklist.

3. Becky uses the short daily meeting to get feedback on how the Plan implementation is going.

4. Becky gives her manager progress reviews during their weekly meetings.

The storm

1. If activities are not getting done fast enough, Becky gets the group together to talk about it.

2. When several employees are given extra work by another department, minor adjustments are made so that the plan's schedule is put back on track.

3. Eventually, Becky hires a temporary worker to help.

Maintain/sustain

1. As they pass each major milestone, Becky's department celebrates in a different way. Becky also keeps the momentum going with frequent and small inspirational updates.

2. Becky maintains her own enthusiasm for the project.

Exercise: How are you going to implement your plan? Write down what you will do for each phase of implementation.

What I'm going to do during the *start*:

1. ________________________________

2. ________________________________

3. ________________________________

What I'm going to do during the *storm*:

1. ______________________________

2. ______________________________

3. ______________________________

What I'm going to do to *maintain/sustain*:

1. ______________________________

2. ______________________________

3. ______________________________

Follow Up

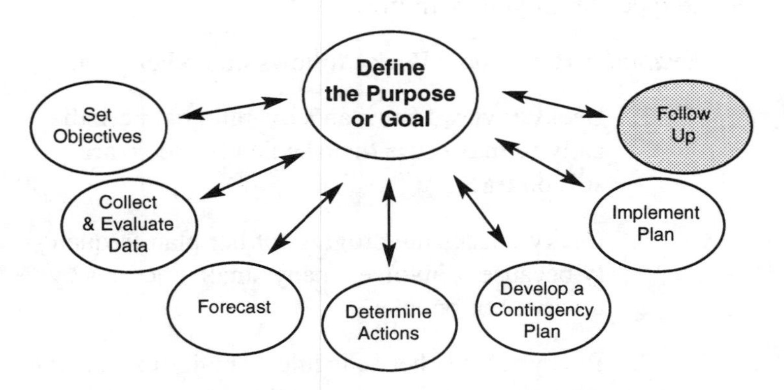

What: Follow-up is a continuous activity. As your plan is implemented, you need to frequently check its progress. The follow-up stage is also where you will determine if any contingency actions are needed. Following up on a plan should be automatic and as frequent as necessary to ensure that your plan is still on course.

How: Check your plan as often as needed. Base your follow-up approach on these criteria:

1. Complexity of the plan — the more complex, the more frequent the follow-ups.

2. Past experience with similar plans — yours and those of others involved.

3. How others think the follow-up should be conducted.

4. The likelihood that contingency plans will be necessary.

Keep in mind that the more specific and measurable your plan, the easier it will be to determine its progress. Also, remember that the overall purpose or goal should still be the focus of all your activities.

Example: Here's how Becky follows up on her plan.

1. Becky reviews her plan's overall goal periodically to make sure that she and her team are still on track.

2. Becky checks the progress of her plan frequently because it involves many smaller actions by a variety of people.

3. Becky revisits her schedule as major milestones are passed, such as when all the processes have been documented.

4. After Becky and her team achieve ISO 9000 certification, they want to assess the plan and its implementation in the interest of continual improvement.

Exercise: What follow-up will be necessary for the plan that you have been working with in this chapter?

1.____

2.____

3.____

Although it seems a bit long and complex, the planning process model will become second nature to you once you have used it a couple of times. It provides busy people with tools that help them maximize their organizational skills while remaining flexible when change inevitably occurs.

Chapter Summary

The planning process model provides a framework for developing single-use plans. The central and starting point in the planning process is always to define the overall purpose or goal of the plan.

The components of the planning process are:

1. Define the overall purpose or goal.
2. Determine the major components or objectives of the plan.
3. Collect and evaluate the data you will need to determine what it will take to complete each component of the plan.
4. Develop a forecast plan.
5. Determine action steps.
6. Develop contingency plans.
7. Implement your plan.
8. Check the progress of your plan frequently.

In general, the more you involve other people in the planning process, the better the plan will be implemented, because everyone will understand and take ownership in the process. During each step of the planning process, refer back to the overall purpose or goal to ensure that your activities are consistent with the desired outcome of your plan.

5 QUALITIES OF A GOOD PLAN

"If you want one year of prosperity, grow grain. If you want 10 years of prosperity, grow trees."

— Chinese Proverb

What makes a plan good or successful? Is it the actual steps that are taken, or is it how the plan is communicated that is most important? The answer is both. Both the tasks and the relationship qualities of your plan must be managed. The tasks are the actual work steps. The relationship qualities include communication, ownership and motivation. By assessing your past and present plans, you can learn how to make your future plans even more effective.

What Makes a Plan Successful?

1. **The plan provides a workable solution.** In other words, plans are made to come to an end. Make sure that your plans provide the structure needed to successfully complete a project or solve a problem!

2. **The plan is comprehensive enough to get the job done right but simple enough to understand and implement.** Plans need to have some structure and should help all those involved keep their focus. On the other hand, a plan that is so detailed that no one wants to use

it will not be very successful. Find out what level of detail is appropriate by talking to the people who actually will use the plan.

3. **The plan minimizes unnecessary or unwanted risks.** With a thorough analysis and good contingency planning, most of the risk will be eliminated. Bear in mind, however, that all plans include some risks.

4. **The plan is specific in terms of time, cost, resources, etc.** The more specific your plan, the better. The people who will use your plan will respond the way you want them to if they are given specific information. Information that is too general breeds behavior that is too general and often off the mark.

5. **The plan is flexible — it can change course if a situation warrants it.** By continually checking your plan's overall purpose or goal, you will be able to make most of the changes needed without negatively affecting its success. Good contingency planning will ensure that you have the resources to make any necessary changes.

6. **The plan was developed using a logical process.** If you are transferred or reassigned during implementation, you want your plan to be so clear that the person taking over for you can easily understand it.

7. **The plan is communicated properly to the people who have to use and support it.** Without their understanding and support, the plan is much more likely to fail.

8. **The plan incorporates the ideas of the people who have to implement and use it.** Again, without their input, the plan will not be as successful.

Example: In the last chapter, Becky put together a plan for getting her department ISO 9000 certified. To find out if she had a good one, she assessed her plan just before she was ready to present it to her managers. Here's what she concluded.

1. **The plan provides a workable solution.** Becky's plan does provide a structured way to get to the desired goal within the stated time frame.

2. **The plan is comprehensive enough to get the job done right but simple enough to understand and implement.** Becky feels that her action plan and forecast are detailed enough to be clear to everyone involved and easy enough to follow.

3. **The plan minimizes unnecessary or unwanted risks.** She feels she did a good job developing contingency plans. Her greatest concern is that not everyone's committed to the plan.

4. **The plan is specific in terms of time, cost, resources, etc.** Becky's action plan and forecast include specifics on time frames, capital and indirect costs associated with the plan and the resources that will be needed to implement it.

5. **The plan is flexible — it can change course if a situation warrants it.** Because she has developed good contingency plans, she feels that her plan is flexible.

6. **The plan was developed using a logical process.** Becky used a logical planning process to develop her plan. Without it, she would have skipped over contingency planning!

7. **The plan is communicated properly to the people who have to use and support it.** Becky has not yet communicated her plan to the people who will use it. She should have communicated it by now, but she hasn't had the time.

8. **The plan incorporates the ideas of the people who have to implement and use it.** Unfortunately, Becky did not involve many people in the development of her plan.

If Becky is smart she will address items 7 and 8 before she presents her plan to her managers!

Is Your Plan A Good One?

Instructions: Answer the following questions to evaluate your plan.

1. Is the overall purpose or goal well defined?

   ____Yes ____No Why?________________

2. Are the right people involved in giving input to your plan?

   ____Yes ____No Why?________________

3. Have you done the necessary data collection to determine what you need to implement your plan?

   ____Yes ____No Why?________________

4. Have you developed a schedule with both linear and concurrent activities?

   ____Yes ____No Why?________________

5. Have you thoroughly explored the "what ifs" and determined contingency actions?

   ____Yes ____No Why?________________

6. Are the people involved in your plan's implementation committed to it?

   ____Yes ____No Why?________________

7 Is the plan realistic?

   ____Yes ____No Why?________________

8. Is the plan measurable in terms of time, costs and resources required?

   ____Yes ____No Why?________________

9. Has the plan been communicated?

   ____Yes ____No Why?________________

10. Was the plan developed using a logical process?

   ____Yes ____No Why?________________

Reflections

Scoring: In general, the more questions you answered yes to, the better your plan is. Unfortunately, answering no to even one question could mean that your plan may be in trouble or may be less successful. Look into those areas that need improvement or clarification.

Chapter Summary

There are several common qualities of good plans. To improve the effectiveness of your future plans, you should continually assess the plans you develop.

It is important to consider both the tasks involved in planning and the relationship qualities: communication, ownership, and motivation.

6 PLANNING FOR CHAOS

"Things which matter most must never be at the mercy of things which matter least."

— Goethe

When the plant automated its 32 manufacturing lines, the jobs of several workers changed. Bob and Sam, both line supervisors, sit at a table in the local watering hole discussing how the changes have affected them.

BOB: *"Sam, I just don't know if I can take it. They tell me that I need to learn how to operate a computer if I want to keep my job."*

SAM: *"Bob, we knew this was coming. Why didn't you get yourself enrolled in the classes at the community college?"*

BOB: *"I'm too old for school."*

SAM: *"Yeah, but you're too young for retirement. Listen, tomorrow I'm going to get a few of the guys together to talk about the new machinery and procedures. Why don't you join us?"*

BOB: *"I'm busy tomorrow."*

SAM: *"Bob, you have to think about which will be more painful — learning a few new procedures or losing your job."*

BOB: *"OK, I'll be there. What time tomorrow?"*

Given today's ever-changing work environment, is it realistic to think that you can bring some order out of chaos? Sure it is! It may not always be easy, but many *changes can be planned.* In fact, you may even learn to like change and actually enjoy its many challenges. To successfully plan for change, you should do the following:

1. Understand how you and those around you respond to change.
2. Understand what behaviors must be modified as a result of the change.
3. Develop a plan for implementing (or participating in) changes.

Understand How You and Those Around You Respond to Change

People tend to either resist or embrace change. When they resist change, it's for many reasons:

- They fear what the change may bring.
- They are comfortable in their current situations.
- They don't understand the change or the reasons for changing.
- They have had bad experiences with past changes.

When people resist change, there are several possible reactions:

- The change is not as successful as planned.
- The people resisting the change are disciplined or fired.
- People who do not resist are also punished because they have to pull more than their fair share of the work.
- The change is not implemented.

People embrace change when:

- They understand the change.
- They receive effective communication about the change.
- They realize the risk of not changing is greater than the risk of accepting the change.

When change is inevitable, you should analyze the factors that influence how people perceive the change. What factors are causing people to resist and how can they overcome them? Obviously, you want to tip the scale in favor of embracing the change! Here are a few ideas:

1. To reduce the fear associated with the change, communicate it as soon as possible and provide frequent updates to supply details and squelch rumors, which are sure to surface. Generally, their fear is really fear of the unknown, so make sure the change is explained well!
2. Involve the very people whom the change will impact in the planning process. People take comfort in being part of the solution.

3. Be sure to explain the reasons behind the change early in the communication process. Why is the change necessary? Make sure you stress the benefits of the change.

4. Hold group meetings to discuss the impact of the change. Often people will feel more comfortable speaking up and asking questions when they are among peers.

5. If an employee strongly resists the change, talk with her one-on-one. Try to understand what the issue is and address it. Often the employee will tell you what needs to be done to make her comfortable with the change.

Understand What Behaviors Must Be Modified as a Result of the Change

Change usually requires you to modify old behaviors or thoughts about something. This behavior transition takes place on two levels: attitudes and knowledge/skills.

Knowledge/skills

Knowledge means acquiring an *understanding* of the change and its components. Proper training and communication are crucial at this level. Skill involves proficiently performing the new behaviors or thoughts that the change requires. Acquiring them depends on the quality of the initial training and your ability to put these new skills or behaviors into practice.

Attitudes

Attitudes also need to be altered when changes occur. The change will be complete and successful only if employees *feel* that the change is beneficial. If their own needs are met somehow during the change, then their attitudes about the change will tend to be more positive. If they do not feel that their needs are served by the change, then their attitudes will be more negative. Keep in mind that their *needs* may be as basic as actually being involved in the change process or helping to establish new procedures related to the change.

Clearly, attitudes are more difficult to change than knowledge and skills. Involving employees in the change process as soon as possible will help those negative attitudes surface, giving you a better chance to deal with them.

Develop a Plan for Implementing Change

In addition to using the planning process described in Chapter 4, you can take other steps to adjust for change.

1. Define the change as specifically as possible. How will this change impact others? What is the desired outcome? Why is the change necessary or advantageous? How will this change allow the company to achieve its objectives?

2. Describe the forces resisting the change as well as those that may pave the way toward easily accepting the change. It pays to enlist the help of friends and foes. You should involve others when gathering this information.

3. Determine how you will address the behavioral changes needed at both the knowledge/skill level and the attitude level. You should understand your employees' current skill levels and what skills are required to implement the

change successfully. Assess the work climate to determine what attitudinal changes are necessary.

4. Determine how the change should be implemented — either all at once or a little at a time. Often the nature of the change will determine how fast it should be implemented. Compare this change to similar past changes to get an idea of how the workforce will respond. Be sensitive to the needs of those impacted by the change — don't overwhelm them.

Case Study

Mark is a department supervisor for the accounting division of a middle-sized company. The department is made up of eight long-term employees who are "used to each other" and who are happy that not too many changes have occurred over the last couple of years. Mark has just gotten the news that his department will take over the accounting work for a newly acquired division within three months. He is in charge of planning all aspects of this change.

For example, the department will get new equipment to help it handle the increased complexity and amount of work, as well as three to five new people, who must be hired and trained. Several of the current accounting processes will be changed to fit the new requirements of both divisions.

Mark knows that his present employees will worry about the changes. They will fear the possibility of having to work longer hours. They also may be concerned about the new equipment and work processes. However, Mark realizes that it is important for them to feel confident about working with new processes, to be committed to the change and to accept the new personnel.

Case study questions

1. When should Mark break the news and how?

   ____

2. How should he deal with his employees' fears about new personnel?

   ____

3. What can he do to increase their confidence?

   ____

4. How can he gain their commitment to the new project?

   ____

5. Based on the available information, determine the resisting factors, develop a sample overall purpose and determine the objectives or major components of the plan to fit Mark's situation.

The resisting factors: __________________________

____

Overall purpose: ______________________________

____

Objectives:

1. ______________________________

2. ______________________________

3. ______________________________

4. ______________________________

5. ______________________________

Exercise: Think about a change that you will need to plan for and answer the following questions.

The change I must plan for: ______________________

1. How do you think people will react to this change? ______________________

   ____

   Will they resist it? Why or why not?

   ____

   ____

   Will they embrace it? Why or why not?

   ____

   ____

2. What can you do to reduce the resisting factors and enhance the reasons for embracing it?

   ____

   ____

3. What behaviors will have to be modified as a result of this change — knowledge/skills and/or attitudes?

   ____

   ____

4. How will you go about modifying these behaviors?

   ____

   ____

5. How will you go about planning for this change? What steps will you follow?

   ____

   ____

Chapter Summary

Many changes can be planned. It is important to understand how people will resist the change and then determine the reasons why they should embrace the change rather than resist it. Most importantly, communicate all aspects of the change. When changes do occur, they require behavioral changes at two levels: knowledge/skill and attitudes.

7 PRESENTING YOUR PLAN

"The few projects in my study that disintegrated did so because the manager failed to build a coalition of supporters and collaborators."

— Rosabeth Moss Kanter *(The Change Masters)*

Once you've come up with a plan, you have to present it to others to gain their commitment, ownership, or approval. Unfortunately, even the best plans can be rejected if they are not presented well. So ask yourself, "What is the purpose of this presentation?" Do you want to gain commitment? Are you seeking approval? Are you looking for input? As you develop your presentation, check periodically to ensure that you are focusing on your defined purpose or goal. This chapter gives you several suggestions and ideas for presenting plans.

An Interesting Opening Statement

You want to create interest in your plan, even if the audience already agrees that it is needed. This does not mean that you want to "beat a dead horse" or "preach to the choir." Still, you should present your plan clearly, concisely, and convincingly.

The interest or opening statement establishes the theme and tone of the presentation. It can be as short or lengthy as needed. If the audience knows about the topic, keep it short.

However, if you are presenting information that the audience is not familiar with, allow more time.

An interest statement should include the following elements:

1. Grab the audience's attention!

   Example 1: "There's more bureaucratic red tape coming our way!"

   Example 2: "Folks, the competition is starting to kill us!"

2. Get agreement on the issue, change the problem that requires the plan of action.

   Example 1: "You have all heard about the new government regulations requiring us to implement new safety procedures." (This audience is very aware of the topic.)

   Example 2: "Over the last three months we have lost customers to the new store down the road. Here are some figures that compare this quarter's profits with those of a year ago." (This audience is not so aware of the topic.)

3. State, in general terms, the approach that your plan will take. Setting a tone should reduce the number of questions that the audience will have, because you are letting them know what you intend to address.

   Example 1: "We need to comply with these new regulations in such a way that they only minimally disrupt our productivity."

Example 2: "While it's true that we need to take a look at offering competitive services, we do not want to blow recent events out of proportion."

4. Provide an overview on how you will proceed with the presentation. Include the time allotted, how you will deal with questions and any other applicable information.

   Example 1: "Over the next 30 minutes, I will present the plan that my team has developed to satisfy both our regulatory commitments and our productivity concerns. We also will briefly review the new regulations. Then we have allotted 10 minutes at the end to answer your questions."

   Example 2: "For the next hour we will look at three possible plans of action that address our recent loss of business. Feel free to ask questions any time during the presentation."

   Complete interest statement for Example 1: (This audience is very aware of the topic.) "There's more bureaucratic red tape coming our way! You have all heard about the new government regulations requiring us to implement new safety procedures. We need to comply with these new regulations in such a way that they only minimally disrupt our productivity. Over the next 30 minutes, I will present the plan that my team has developed to satisfy both our regulatory commitments and our productivity concerns. We also will briefly review the new regulations. Then we have allotted 10 minutes at the end to answer your questions."

Complete interest statement for Example 2:
(This audience is not so aware of the topic.)
"Folks, the competition is starting to kill us! Over the last three months we have lost customers to the new store down the road. Here are some figures that compare this quarter's profits with those of a year ago. While it's true that we need to take a look at offering competitive services, we do not want to blow recent events out of proportion. For the next hour we will look at three possible plans of action that address our recent loss of business. Feel free to ask questions any time during the presentation."

As you can see, both of these interest statements ask for agreement from the audience, state the approach the plan will take and then provide an overview of the presentation.

Broad View

After an opening, begin your presentation by discussing the broad view of your topic, your approach to the planning process, and the plan itself. There are two reasons why starting with a broad view makes sense.

1. You want to establish an overall understanding of your plan. If you start the presentation by projecting your schedule or action plan on an overhead screen, you run the risk of confusing the audience. As a result, you probably will get lots of questions that could have been avoided.

2. By presenting the broad view first, you can "read" your audience to see how much detail members want to hear. Often the broad view is enough to fulfill the needs of the audience. You want to give only the level of detail that is necessary. If one or two people want to see the details of the plan, invite them to a one-on-one meeting at a later time.

In presenting the broad view, make sure it contains these four components:

1. Summarize the issue, problem or change that triggered your plan. Make sure audience members understand the overall situation.

   Example 1: "Last January, the state passed a group of laws requiring ... Currently, our procedures are such that ... So that's the situation we're in. Is everybody clear on this?"

   Example 2: "I've briefly touched on this quarter's financial results; now let's look at the situation a little more closely ... So, you see, we are being impacted in more ways than one ... Does anyone have any questions about the current situation?"

2. Describe how you and/or your group developed the plan. How did you conduct the necessary research, what processes did you use, what overall conclusions did you make?

   Example 1: "To determine the best course of action, we talked to the employees who will be impacted and three other local companies. We brainstormed alternatives and then narrowed down that list based on overall cost and impact on quality ... Based on our analysis, we have determined ..."

Example 2: "First, we defined what the customer wants by sending out surveys. Here's what we found ... When we compared our services to these customers' requirements, three major issues surfaced ... After assessing our existing resources, we determined the best overall actions would be to ..."

3. Describe the overall purpose or goal of your plan and its major components. Also, briefly discuss any major contingency plans. State the overall time frame and resources needed to implement the plan.

   Example 1: "The purpose of our plan is to ... This can be broken into six major objectives ... Because this is a new regulation we considered what we'd do if ... Here's how the action plan and forecast look ..."

   Example 2: "Bottom-line, our goal is to update our product selection and speed of service ... To do this we will need to achieve the following objectives ... Our plan is based on a prediction that consumer spending will rise. To take advantage of this projection we feel we need to execute the plan within the next six months. As our action plan shows ..."

4. Describe the desired outcome in terms of how the environment will "look" when your plan is complete.

   Example 1: "Successful implementation of our plan will result in total state compliance with only a 2 percent decrease in overall productivity."

Example 2: "Within one year we should be able to service the customer within two days while offering 12 new products. We feel that this achievement will increase our market share and our profitability."

Measuring the Success of Your Plan

It is important that the audience members understand how you will track your plan. They need to know that if things go wrong, then any problems will be addressed immediately. To communicate that you are "on top of things," during your presentation include information on the following topics:

1. How will you know if the plan is working?

   Example 1: "We will conduct internal audits every month, measuring both compliance and productivity. This will ensure that we are on target with our plan."

   Example 2: "Our plan is to perform weekly customer surveys and daily service-time measurements to track our progress."

2. What are the major milestones of your plan (critical measurements)?

   Example 1: "Our interim goals are ..."

   Example 2: "To achieve our overall goal we need to see monthly improvements in these areas ..."

3. How will you communicate the plan's progress (weekly, daily, monthly updates, etc.)?

   Example 1: "We will update you on our progress at the monthly staff meetings."

   Example 2: "We've established a place on the bulletin board where we can post daily sales totals and weekly customer survey results."

4. What are you prepared to do if things go wrong?

   Example 1: "We don't anticipate any problems, but if we cannot maintain our productivity targets while making these changes, we will get the group back together immediately to determine what's not working."

   Example 2: "Although we are confident that our plan will work, we will certainly alert you right away if we don't see the kinds of improvements we predict. At that point, we might have to radically rethink our strategies."

Communicating the Details

Most audiences will want to see your schedule (forecast) and your action plan. Beyond those two items, the amount of detail that you offer depends on the audience. Present your action plan first and then your schedule. Let any other details come out in the question-and-answer period following your presentation. Provide details in a way that simply summarizes each major component of your plan.

Example 1: "Here's our overall action plan ... And the schedule looks like this ..."

Example 2: "Based on what we have talked about so far, here's how our plan looks from a division-of-work perspective. (Show action plan and explain briefly.) We think that the following time schedule is realistic ..."

Next Steps

To make your presentation a success, you need to be clear about what you expect the audience to do next and what you and/or your team will do next. Those actions that you and your team will take should be presented in a general fashion, without too much detail. If you expect the audience to act, get agreement on how members want to accomplish their assignments. This requires a more detailed approach as well as follow-up on your part.

Example 1: "So, if all of us are in agreement, here's what has to be done next ... This is the support we need from you ... Here's what the team needs to do next ..."

Example 2: "Because there's a lot that each area has to do, we'd like each of you to take this information back to your department, review it with your employees, and decide if it's realistic. We'll meet again at the end of the week to discuss your findings."

Questions and Answers

Always allow a few minutes at the end of your presentation for questions, even if you have answered questions along the way. (There are always some people who will wait to hear the entire presentation before asking any questions.) Most presenters have no problem dealing with the informational aspect of answering questions about their plans; that is, they have the *knowledge* to answer them. However, many have difficulty with the *emotional* aspect of answering questions, because they feel the audience is challenging their authority, preparedness or the quality of their plans. Here are a few tips:

1. Don't take the questions too seriously or personally! Often people are personally offended when their plans are criticized. Keep in mind that everyone has an opinion *and everyone generally wants to share it.* If your stomach knots up when people make suggestions regarding your work, you will tend to show it physically through a lack of facial expressions, being nonparticipative, a sweaty brow, etc. Eventually people will give up trying to contribute.

2. Invite ideas and suggestions. An idea improves only with someone else's input — *really.*

3. Ask a trusted peer to give you feedback on how well you handle answering questions about your plan.

4. Pause a couple of seconds before responding to a question. This will help you resist the urge to immediately respond in a defensive manner. Also, by asking clarifying follow-up questions, you communicate that you are open-minded. Here are some examples:

"Are you interested in hearing more about our customer research or the competitive research?"

"So your question is whether the money is going to be available in time to implement the project, right?"

"Tell me a little more about what you're getting at."

Preparing Handout Materials

What you hand out during your presentation is as important as what you say. Your handouts should be clear and concise but not too detailed. For the most effective handout, include these elements:

1. *Cover sheet*: Your cover sheet should state the name or topic of the plan, the purpose of the presentation, your and/or your group's name(s) and the presentation date. Here's an example:

   Presentation: Meeting New Government Safety Regulations

   Today's Purpose: To present a proposed action plan and gain the necessary approval to move forward

   Presented by: R. Smith, J. Coop, M. Mena

   October 20, 2000

2. *Synopsis of presentation*: In your handout, outline the main points of your presentation in the same order as they are presented. Clearly differentiate each major section of the presentation and use graphics (tables, charts, etc.) and bullet points whenever possible. People absorb infor-

mation better if it is presented in a variety of ways, so combining graphics, written words and your verbal comments will increase the effectiveness of your presentation. Also, using an overhead projector or slides to show your handouts allows people to follow along with your presentation. For example, your presentation synopsis might look like this:

Page 1:	Cover sheet.
Page 2:	Overview statement and information about the current situation that has caused the need for a plan.
Page 3:	Bar graph illustrating the current situation.
Page 4:	Line chart illustrating the current situation.
Page 5:	Overall goal of your plan.
Page 6:	Your plan's main objectives.
Page 7:	Your action plan.
Page 8:	Chart outlining your schedule.
Page 9:	How your plan's success will be measured..
Page 10:	Next steps for you and audience members.
Page 11:	Other information sheet (see next step).

3. *Other information sheet*: Follow the presentation's synopsis with any additional information that the audience needs about the project plan. Include contact names, phone numbers, and where to go for more details, including reference materials.

Chapter Summary

Even the best plans can be rejected if they are not presented well. Your presentation should offer the audience a broad view of your plan. Presentation components include an opening interest statement, a broad view or plan synopsis, plan measurements, plan details and necessary next steps. You should present your plan in a way that is thorough but not too detailed. Your presentation handouts should be professional and concise. They should contain the main points of your presentation in a condensed form. Finally, your presentation should leave the audience members with a clear understanding of the necessary next steps, both for them and for you and your team.

8 PLANNING TOOLS

"Men have become the tools of their tools."

— Henry David Thoreau

Developing a plan involves collecting, organizing and analyzing information. There are several tools that can help you manage all this data. You should understand what each tool does before selecting the right ones to use with your plan. The following chart will help you decide which tool(s) you should use.

If you need to	Then try this tool
Organize individual activities within a plan, including responsibilities and measurements	Action plan, pp. 92-93
Develop a schedule or forecast	Gantt chart, p. 93-94
Collect data	Check sheet, pp. 94-96
Prioritize the plan's impact, problems or issues	Pareto analysis, pp. 96-97
Depict graphically the steps of a process	Flow chart, pp. 97-99
Gather many ideas or thoughts	Brainstorming, pp. 99-100
Analyze a process for improvement	Process improvement, pp. 100-104
Prioritize activities or eliminate activities that don't add value	Value analysis, pp. 104-106

Throughout this chapter are examples of these tools, which you may use when developing your own plans.

Action Plan

What: Use action plans to ensure that each step of your plan is completed successfully. With a solid action plan, all members of a team know exactly what needs to be done, by whom and by when.

How: Use action plans every time you must implement a plan! Action plans can be used for most plans.

Action Plan					
Project:				Project Leader:	
Overall Purpose:					
Step No.	Action Step	Start	End	Measurement Criteria	Responsibility of

Action plan tips

1. Good action plans are time-based.
2. Good action plans state the overall purpose or goal statement.

3. Good action plans rely on consensus from all members of the implementation team.

4. Good action plans include measurements to track the plan.

5. Good action plans allow for some flexibility in how their steps are accomplished.

6. Good action plans hold everyone involved accountable for their actions and responsibilities.

Gantt Chart

What: A Gantt chart is a type of scheduling tool that displays the starts, finishes and durations of activities as activity bars placed along a time line to visually monitor a project's progress.

How: Gantt charts can be used whenever a project has several major components or milestones (interim goal points) that must be tracked on a time schedule. (An example of the Gantt chart Becky used for her plan to get her department ISO 9000 certified appears on p. 47.)

Gantt chart tips

1. Get input from others who have a good understanding of the plan's major components.

2. Be sure to document all the tasks needed to complete the plan. Record these along the left-hand column of the chart, putting them in the approximate order that they need to be done.

3. Indicate major milestones in linear progression of tasks.

Project Time Line (in ____________)

Objectives/tasks							

Check Sheet

What: Use check sheets to gather data that show how often, where, and when certain events occur, particularly errors, defects, variations, or process failures. Check sheets translate your opinions about a problem or situation into facts, so data patterns become obvious very quickly.

How: Use check sheets when developing a problem-solving plan that requires you to collect data.

Check Sheet

Project: Project Leader:

Definition of the information being collected:

Reason/Activity	Dates																				

Check sheet tips

1. Agree on what the check sheet will capture. What events are you looking for? Be specific.
2. Determine the time period in which the data will be collected. When will the collection period begin and end? Will measurements be made hourly, daily, weekly, etc.?
3. Create the check sheet. Is it easy to understand and use? Does it capture all the needed information?
4. Collect the data. Be consistent and unbiased. Allow adequate time for accurate data collection.
5. To collect accurate data, you must feel confident about recording the bad news as well as

the good. Don't try to sugarcoat the truth to please upper management.

Pareto Analysis

What: A Pareto analysis is a special type of vertical bar chart that visually compares numerical data, usually check sheet information. It displays from greatest to least how often things happen, such as types of problems, costs of problems, problems by product, or any other measurements that help identify the most significant problems. A Pareto analysis will help you focus your efforts on problems that have the greatest potential for improvement.

How: Use Pareto analysis to prioritize problems or identify issues that must be addressed. For example, you might use Pareto analysis to decide which of your department's processes need the most improvement.

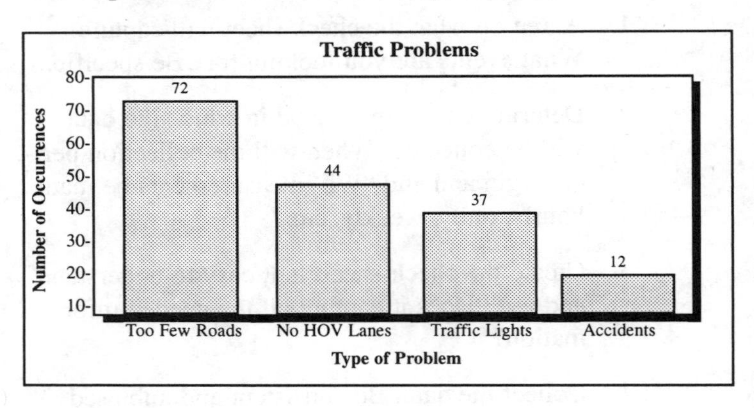

Pareto analysis tips

1. Decide which problem you want to know more about.

2. Make sure that the possible causes of the problem are measurable.

3. List the problem categories on the horizontal line and frequencies on the vertical line.

4. Carefully interpret the results. What does this data mean with regard to your project plan?

Flow Chart

What: Flow charts are graphs that clearly show the sequence of steps in a process and the relationships among these steps.

How: Use flow charts to document, analyze or develop a sequence of activities or steps in a process, either actual or ideal. For process improvement activities flow charts can help uncover delays and/or non-value-added activities. Flow charting is also useful for uncovering unexpected complexities in a process because you often don't know what steps are involved until you chart them out!

Definition of symbols:

- Circle: beginning or end point of a process
- Rectangle: process step
- Diamond: decision point, usually a question answered by yes or no
- Arrows: indicate the flow of the process

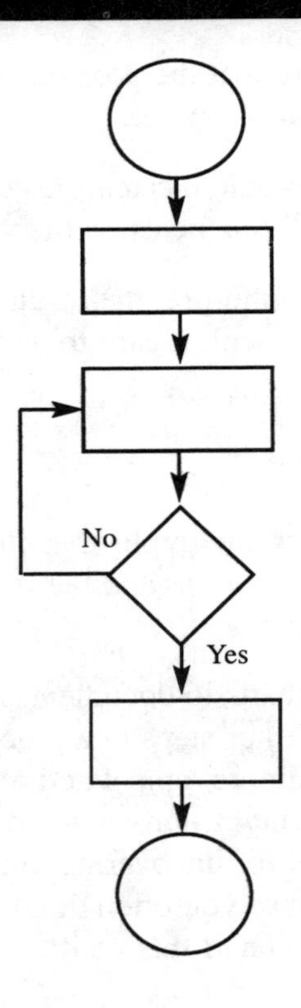

Flow chart tips

1. Determine the appropriate starting and ending points of the process being evaluated.
2. Don't use a flow chart on too big a process. Break it down into subprocesses.
3. Ask "What happens next?"
4. Keep the flow chart clear and simple.
5. Verify the processes with the people who perform those activities.

6. Indicate decision steps and feedback loops (points where the process returns to an earlier step).
7. Be consistent in the level of detail shown.
8. Test your flow chart for completeness.

Brainstorming

What: Brainstorming is a highly versatile tool that uses the creativity of a group to generate a large volume of ideas for a project or to solve a problem. Participants share their ideas spontaneously through free association within a "safe" environment, where their ideas won't be challenged or ridiculed. Brainstorming encourages open thinking when a team is stuck in the status quo.

How: Brainstorming has a multitude of applications within the project-planning and problem-solving processes. It is an important tool in creating action plans and contingency plans.

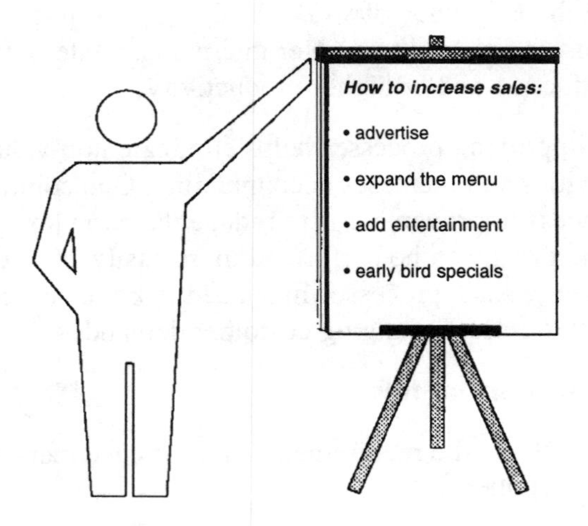

Brainstorming tips

1. The central brainstorming questions should be stated, agreed on, and written down on a flip chart or blackboard for everyone to see.
2. Ask each person to offer one idea at a time.
3. Record all ideas.
4. Avoid both criticism and praise of ideas.
5. Strive for full participation.
6. Don't quit too soon.
7. Encourage creativity and breakthrough thinking.
8. Have fun.

Process Improvement

What: Process improvement is used to determine how to increase the efficiency of work. Analyzing and improving these processes can lead to greater internal and external customer satisfaction and/or higher productivity.

How: Improving processes helps eliminate non-value-added activities and increases accountability. One common goal of process improvement is to reduce the complexity of a process so that it can be performed more easily, efficiently and effectively. Also, processes may need to be reworked periodically to reflect changing customer demands.

Process improvement tips

1. Define the requirements of your customers and suppliers.

2. Make sure that inputs and outputs can be clearly measured.

3. Identify value-added and non-value-added activities.

4. Be sure that your processes are flexible and responsive to changing conditions.

5. Define what you want to gain by improving the process. Will the benefits outweigh the costs of improvements?

6. Involve all employees who use the process in the improvement plan.

7. Don't point fingers at people; instead, focus on the process.

8. Break the process down into subprocesses if it is too large or complex.

9. Rely on facts and data, not on assumptions and perceptions.

Process improvement steps

1. Plan what you want to improve. High-impact, low-productivity processes are among the best candidates for process improvement.

2. Prepare a team to work on the process improvement.

3. Document the process. (See the flow chart section of this chapter.)

4. Clarify what the process is supposed to do (customer requirements). Talk to customers directly

and involve them in the processes to ensure that any changes meet their requirements.

5. Measure and monitor the process. Establish a goal for what you want to measure.

    - Collect data. (See the check sheet and Pareto analysis sections of this chapter.)

    - Compare your measurement to customers' requirements.

6. Analyze the process.

    - Look for non-value-added activities.

    - Look for redundancies.

    - Look for ways to streamline the process.

    - Determine which steps to keep and which steps to eliminate in the process. If there are gaps in the process, steps may need to be added.

    - Develop a goal statement for the improvement plan using the following format: "To (increase/decrease) the (output/measurement) from (current performance) to (preferred performance) by (date)."

7. Apply problem-solving to areas that need improvement. This may include forming subteams for particularly large processes.

Process Improvement Worksheet

(Insert a flow chart of your process here.)

Process strengths (keep doing, maximize):

____

____

Process weaknesses (do better, strengthen):

____

____

____

Non-value-added process activities (stop doing, minimize):

____

____

Process gaps (start doing, address, resolve):

___

___

___

Value Analysis

What: A value analysis is a critical examination of activities done by a group or an individual to determine which add value to the organization. The goal of a value analysis is to uncover tasks that can be eliminated or reduced, especially when you need to cut costs, prioritize better, or take on new projects.

How: Here are the steps for completing a value analysis. Use the worksheet that follows to record your work.

1. List the tasks that you do (or that the work group does) in the column labeled TASK.
2. Define why the task is done in the column labeled WHY DONE?
3. Rate the impact that the task has on the organization in terms of its strategic goals and objectives. A rating of 1 means no impact, while a rating of 10 means extremely high impact.
4. Rate how resource-intensive the task is (money, time, people required). A rating of 1 means little to no resources required, while a rating of 10 means many resources are needed.
5. Indicate if the task is required by some oversight organization (corporate office; federal,

state or local laws; government agencies; etc.). These tasks probably can't be eliminated.

Value Analysis Worksheet				
Task	Why Done?	Impact? (1-10)	Resource-Intensive? (1-10)	Required?

Based on your analysis, answer the following questions:

1. Are there any tasks that could be eliminated or reduced? Concentrate your analysis on those activities that are very resource-intensive but have little impact.
2. Are there any tasks that should be automated?
3. Are there any tasks that should be modified?
4. Are there any tasks that should be done more frequently or with more resources dedicated to them? Concentrate on those activities that have a great deal of impact on your organization.

Work Equation

Focus on value-added activities and reduce organizational hassles (non-value added work).

	Activities that are done today
+	Tasks that need to be added (high value-adding tasks)
–	Tasks that need to be deleted (low value-adding tasks)
=	Maximum-value activities

After completing a work equation, answer these questions:

1. Did you tend to leave out parts of the equation? Which one(s)?
2. Which part of the equation is most difficult to define?
3. How should you determine which activities go and which stay?

Chapter Summary

When you develop a plan, you need to collect and/or analyze data. Knowing the right tool to use is very important. You should choose a tool based on the type of information you need. Tools that help busy people with their plans include action plans, Gantt charts, check sheets, Pareto analysis, flow charts, brainstorming, process improvement, and value analysis.

While the planning process may seem a bit tedious and time-consuming at first, it will fast become second nature to you. By following the tips and techniques outlined in this handbook, you ensure that every project you undertake gets off to a good start and then stays on track.

SUGGESTED READING

Brassard, Michael, Diane Ritter. *The Memory Jogger II*. Methuen, MA: Goal/QPC, 1994.

Covey, Stephen. *The 7 Habits of Highly Effective People*. New York: Simon & Schuster, 1989.

Davis, Brian et al. *Successful Manager's Handbook*. New York: Personnel Decisions, Inc., 1992.

Drucker, Peter. *The Practice of Management*. New York: Harper & Row, 1954.

Fink, Steven. *Crisis Management: Planning for the Inevitable*. New York: AMACOM, 1986.

Halloran, Jack, George Frunzi. *Supervision: The Art of Management*. Englewood Cliffs, NJ: Prentice Hall, 1986.

Kaufman, Roger. *Strategic Planning Plus: An Organizational Guide*. Glenview, IL: Foresman and Company, 1991.

Macdonald, Chris. *The Productive Supervisor: Planning Skills*. Amherst, MA: Human Resource Development Press, 1985.

Makridakis, Spyros G. *Forecasting, Planning and Strategy for the 21st Century*. New York: The Free Press, 1990.

Manning, Marilyn, Patricia Haddock. *Leadership Skills for Women*. Menlo Park, CA: Crisp Publications, 1989.

Miller, Jack, Mary Porter. *Supervision in the Hospitality Industry*. New York: John Wiley & Sons, 1985.

Senge, Peter et al. *The Fifth Discipline Fieldbook*. New York: Doubleday, 1994.

Van Dersal, William. *The Successful Supervisor in Government and Business*. New York: Harper & Row, 1985.

INDEX

P

NOTES

Notes